Excel
Basic Skills

Problem Solving

3-4 Years
Ages
8-10

Get the Results You Want!

3 Johns

PASCAL PRESS

ISBN 978 1 74020 050 9

Pascal Press
PO Box 250
Glebe NSW 2037
(02) 8585 4044
www.pascalpress.com.au

Published by Vivienne Joannou
Edited by Beverley Weynton
Text design and typesetting by Tarnie Lowson
Cover by DiZign Pty Ltd
Printed by Vivar Printing/Green Giant Press

Contents

Year 3

Year 4

Introduction

This book provides an innovative approach to mathematical problem solving, and is designed to give Year 3 and Year 4 children the opportunity to practise problem-solving skills that have been taught at school. The book is divided into two sections: Year 3 and Year 4. Each section is divided into self-contained units, with easy-to-understand explanations and interesting activities. Students should be able to use the book without supervision, and parents should be able to use it as a guide to explaining problem-solving concepts.

The Year 3 units are made up of an explanation page with worked examples, followed by one page of activities relating to the particular problem-solving strategy. The Year 4 units have three pages of activities. All the activities involve problems that relate to children's everyday experiences, so they can easily visualise such situations. Both sections contain four revision tests to complete along the way and answers are supplied in a convenient lift-out section.

Finding a Pattern

1. Let's look at some picture patterns first.

Ducks on the pond

Monday

☆ The number of ducks changed each day.

☆ How did it change?

Tuesday

☆ Look down the column to find the change each day.

Wednesday

On Monday	- 3 ducks.
On Tuesday	- 4 ducks.
On Wednesday	- 5 ducks.
On Thursday	- 3 ducks again.

Thursday

☆ What is the pattern?

☆ The pattern is **3, 4, 5**.

Friday

☆ If Thursday is once again 3 ducks, then the number on Friday is 4.

Shape Patterns

2. There is a pattern in this column of shapes. Look down the column to identify the pattern.

 The first circle has 5 dots.

 This circle has 4 dots.

 This circle has 3 dots.

 Once again, the circle has 5 dots.
The pattern then is **5 dots, 4 dots, 3 dots**.

 If the pattern is 5, 4, 3, then the number of dots here must be 4.
The answer is 4 dots.

Activities

Complete the last picture on each line. Always look for the pattern.
Once you have identified the pattern, decide on the final drawing.

1. Complete these patterns.

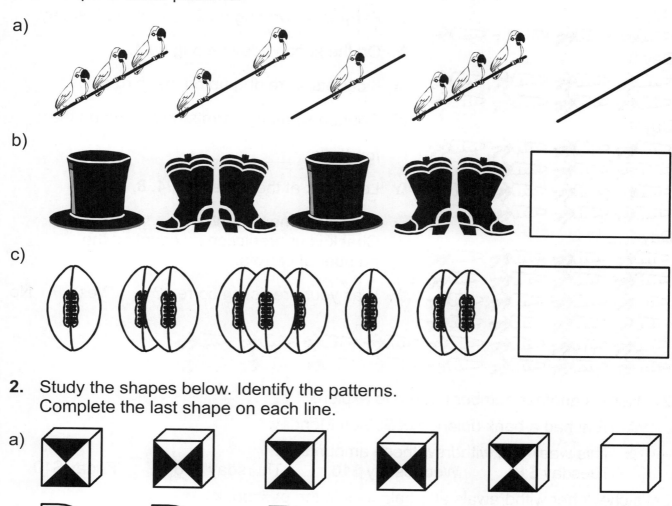

a)

b)

c)

2. Study the shapes below. Identify the patterns.
Complete the last shape on each line.

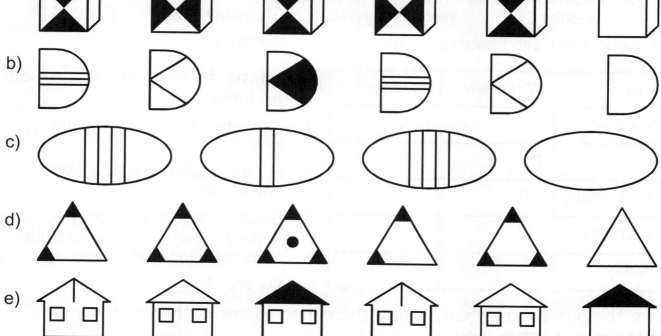

a)

b)

c)

d)

e)

Finding a Pattern

1. Let's check out these number patterns.

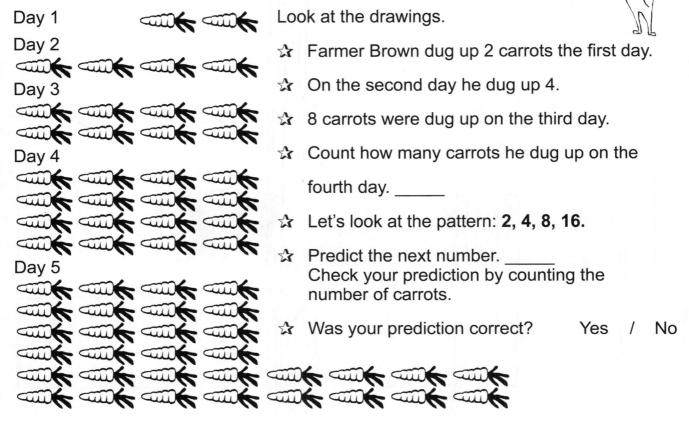

Day 1

Day 2

Day 3

Day 4

Day 5

Look at the drawings.

☆ Farmer Brown dug up 2 carrots the first day.

☆ On the second day he dug up 4.

☆ 8 carrots were dug up on the third day.

☆ Count how many carrots he dug up on the fourth day. _____

☆ Let's look at the pattern: **2, 4, 8, 16.**

☆ Predict the next number. _____
Check your prediction by counting the number of carrots.

☆ Was your prediction correct?   Yes   /   No

2. Here is another number pattern to explore.

☆ Toni had a bank balance of $96 on Monday.

☆ This week she withdrew these amounts:
Tuesday $10,   Wednesday $10,   Thursday $10,   Friday $10.

Let's check her withdrawals and balances in the passbook.

Day	Withdrew	Balance
Monday		$96
Tuesday	$10	$86
Wednesday	$10	$76
Thursday		
Friday		

Complete the missing withdrawals in the book.

There are two ways of finding the balance.

a) For each balance subtract the amount withdrawn; or

b) Because a pattern is being formed (by withdrawing the same amount) follow that pattern:

96, 86, 76, _____, _____.

Use the pattern method to find the other balances then check your pattern by subtracting.

Activities

1. Predict the next elements in these patterns. Colour or draw to show the patterns.

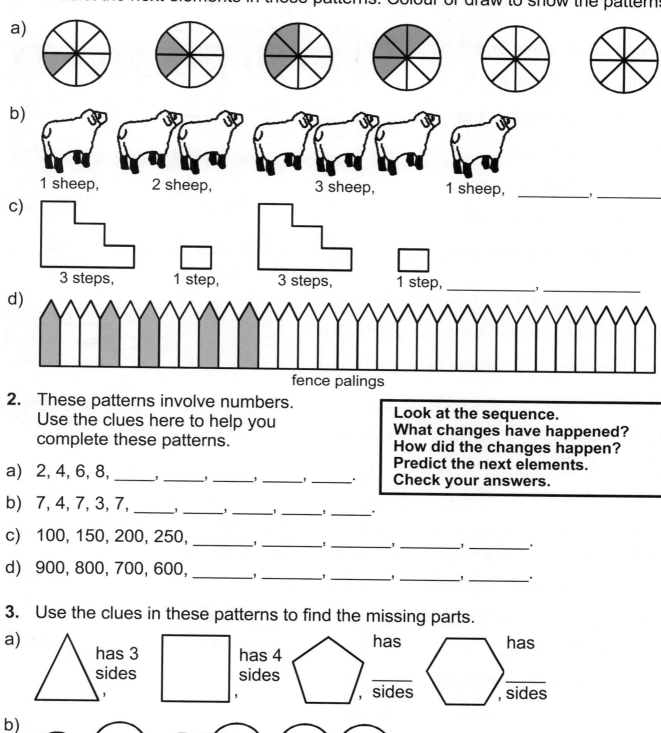

a)

b)

1 sheep,　　　　2 sheep,　　　　　　3 sheep,　　　　　1 sheep, _____ , _____

c)

3 steps,　　　1 step,　　　3 steps,　　　1 step, _____ , _____

d)

fence palings

2. These patterns involve numbers. Use the clues here to help you complete these patterns.

> Look at the sequence.
> What changes have happened?
> How did the changes happen?
> Predict the next elements.
> Check your answers.

a) 2, 4, 6, 8, _____, _____, _____, _____, _____.

b) 7, 4, 7, 3, 7, _____, _____, _____, _____, _____.

c) 100, 150, 200, 250, _____, _____, _____, _____, _____.

d) 900, 800, 700, 600, _____, _____, _____, _____, _____.

3. Use the clues in these patterns to find the missing parts.

a) has 3 sides ,　　has 4 sides ,　　has ____ sides ,　　has ____ sides

b) 10 ¢ , 20 ¢ , 10 ¢ , 20 ¢ , 20 ¢ , 20 ¢ _____, _____, _____, _____

c) ☺ , ☹ , ☹ , ☺ , ☹ , ☹ , _____, _____, _____, _____, _____

Drawing a Picture

1. Drawing a picture can help you solve some problems. Check out this problem.

There are 5 boys and 7 girls.

☆ Tom plays football.

☆ Mary plays football, too.

☆ Jim plays no sport.

☆ All the other boys play cricket.

☆ Tina plays cricket also.

☆ The other girls play only netball.

a) Let's draw in the boys and girls.

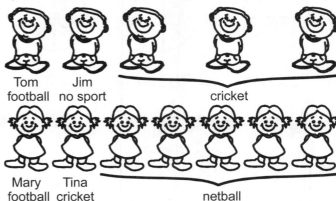

Tom — football
Jim — no sport
cricket

Mary — football
Tina — cricket
netball

b) Name the people we know and the sports they play.

c) Now we have a much better idea, so let's tackle the questions.

i) How many children do not play any sport? _____

ii) There are _____ children who play cricket.

iii) The footballers' names are _____ and _____.

iv) There are more / less netballers than cricketers.

v) Find these totals: no sport _____   cricket players _____

footballers _____   netballers _____

See how a drawing can help you SEE the problem!
Words can be confusing; drawings make things easier.

2. Solve this problem by completing the drawing.

There were 3 birds on each branch.

There are 4 branches.

Five birds flew away. How many are left?

a) Draw in all of the birds on the branches.

b) Place an X on the birds that flew away.

c) Now calculate the number of birds remaining. _____

d) If only 2 birds flew away, what would the total number of birds be if 4 birds joined those sitting on the branches? _____

Activities

Solve these problems by drawing a sketch or diagram.

Problem	Sketch/Diagram	Answer
a) I had a bucket holding 10 litres of water. 2 litres spilled out. 1 litre leaked out through a tiny hole. How much have I left in the bucket to water my plants?		
b) A wall is 6 metres long. How many chairs, each 60 cm wide, can I place side-by-side along this wall?		
c) In a race, Jill crossed the finish line in second place. Tom was 2 metres behind Jill. Mary was 3 metres in front of Tom. Scott was 1 metre behind Tom. Scott was 1 metre behind Tom. Work out who came first, second, third and fourth.		
d) I have four posters to hang on my bedroom wall. Show at least 4 ways I could arrange them.		
e) Mrs Tesch has offered to transport her son's cricket team to the oval for the game. There are 11 boys. How many trips will she need to make if her car can carry 5 people? (Be careful! Don't forget that Mrs Tesch must be included in the 5 people.)		

Drawing a Sketch

1. Sketches can be used to show different arrangements. Here are 3 children: Mike, Carly and Vanessa. Show all of the possible arrangements.

| Here's one way. | Here's another. | This is a third way. |

| Mike | Carly | Vanessa | Mike | Vanessa | Carly | Vanessa | Mike | Carly |

Write the names under the sketches. There is a total of _____ ways.

2. I have 4 coins – 10 cents, 20 cents, 50 cents and one dollar.

| Here is one possible arrangement. | Here is another. |

Your task is to show 10 other ways.

a)	f)
b)	g)
c)	h)
d)	i)
e)	j)

Activities

1. The Australian flag uses the colours red, white and blue. A blue background with red and white crosses in the top left hand corner, and white stars.

Complete these flags below, using a different arrangement of colours to make new flags.

2. I have a bag containing green and yellow counters. If I take out three – one at a time – and place them on the table, what possible arrangements can I make? One is done for you.

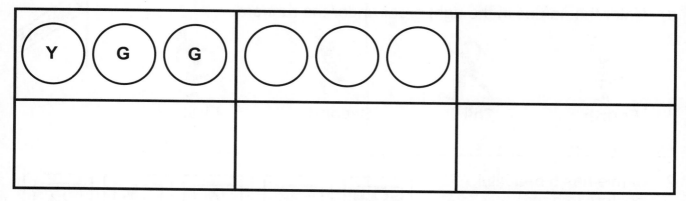

3. Instead of taking out three counters, Julie took out four. Show all of the possible ways her arrangements could be made.

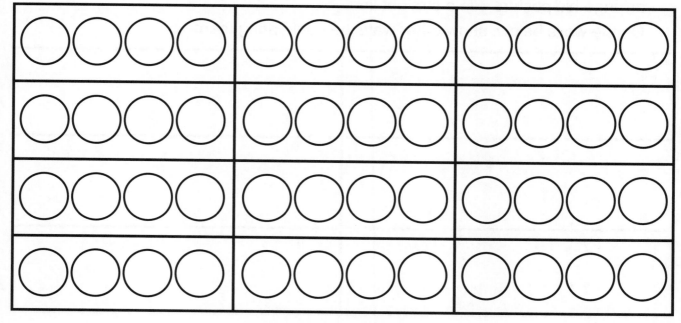

Drawing a Diagram

1. Four children – Anna, Barry, Chris and David were in a race.
   ☆ Anna finished in front of Chris.
   ☆ David did not finish in front of anyone.
   ☆ Chris was in front of Barry.
   ☆ David did not beat Barry.
   ## Let's draw four shapes to represent the runners.

   1.   2.   3.   4.

   a) From the first piece of information, Anna could be 1, 2 or 3.
   b) David can only be last.
   c) If Chris is in front of Barry, then Barry must be 3 and Chris 2, therefore, Anna

   must be _____.
   d) Enter the names in the right order under the runners.

   Fourth   **Third**   **Second**   **First**

   _____   _____   _____   _____

2. Jamie has 5 beautiful posters to hang on his bedroom wall.

   This is one way he could arrange his posters – in a straight line.

   On the walls below, show other ways he could hang them.

Year 3: Unit 2

Activities

Draw the fence here.

1. Jack is building a fence.
The distance between each post is 2 metres.
If he uses 8 posts, how long is the fence?

Answer: The fence is _____ metres long.

2. Tina is building a fence which is 12 metres
long. If the posts are put in every 2 metres,
how many posts will she need?

Answer: The fence needs _____ posts.

3. 32 people were standing in line waiting to
catch taxis.
Each taxi can take 3 passengers.
What is the least number of taxis needed to
transport all these people?
(Hint: Draw 32 people. Group them in 3s.
Count the total number of groupings/part
groupings.)

Answer: _____ taxis will be needed.

4. The ferry across the river can take 8 vehicles
at a time.
There is a line of 27 vehicles waiting to cross.
To clear the line of cars, the ferry will have to
make how many trips?
(Draw the number of cars. Group them in the
number required. This will give you the
number of trips.)

Answer: The ferry must make at least _____
trips.

5. Tanya goes up 2 steps, back one, up 2, back one.
There are 8 steps in total.
How many times will she repeat this until her feet
are on the top step?

Answer: _____ times

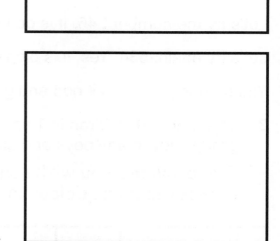

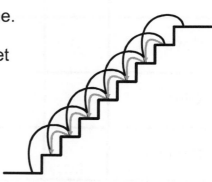

**How much did you learn?
Try the test on page 30.**

Guessing and Checking

1. Taylor has 5 coins - 10 cent and 20 cent coins. The total value is 70 cents. How many of each coin does she have?

   If she has 5 coins it could be 1 ten cent and 4 twenty cent coins.

   $1 \times 10 ¢ = 10 ¢$ $4 \times 20 ¢ = 80 ¢$ $10 ¢ + 80 ¢ = 90 ¢$

   This is not right.

   Let's guess again. 2 ten cent and 3 twenty cent coins.

   $2 \times 10 ¢ = 20 ¢$ $3 \times 20 ¢ = 60 ¢$ $20 ¢ + 60 ¢ = 80 ¢$

   Still not right, but closer to the answer.

   You make a guess.

   _____ ten cent coins   _____ twenty cent coins

   Now check your guess.

   _____ × 10 ¢ = _____   _____ × 20 ¢ = _____   _____ + _____ = _____

   If this guess was not correct, try again.

2. Here are the digits 3, 4 and 5. Your task is to make an odd number greater than 500.

   Let's try the number 345. It is odd but not greater than 500.

   Let's try again. 534. Yes, it is bigger than 500 but it is even, not odd.

   You try one _____. Is it odd and greater than 500?   Yes / No

3. There are 29 children in Tina's class. There are 5 more girls than boys in this group. How many boys and girls are in this class group?

   I've provided you with some guesses. Check them out to find the correct answer. Colour in the correct guess to make it stand out.

Total	29	29	29		29		29	
Boys	6	8	10	13		9		20
Girls					17		14	
Difference								

Activities

1. In the paddock I counted 38 animals. They were sheep and cattle.
There were 8 more sheep than cattle.
How many of each animal were in the paddock?

	1st guess	2nd guess	3rd guess		
Total					
Sheep					
Cattle					
Difference					

Make sure you check each guess. Sheep + cattle must equal 38.
Sheep - cattle must be 8.

2. There are 50 cent and one dollar coins in my pocket. There is double the
number of 50 cent coins than one dollar coins. The total value of all the coins

is $8, so I must have _____ 50 cent coins and _____ one dollar coins.

Use this table to make your guesses. Check each guess. If it is not
correct, use that guess as an idea for another guess. Continue guessing
and checking until you find the right combination.

	1st guess	2nd guess	3rd guess	
50 cent coins	___ × 50¢ = $___			
One dollar coins	___ × $1 = $___			
Total value	$___			

3. If the total value of the coins was $10 not $8, then I would have _____ one

dollar coins and _____ 50 cent coins.

Guess 1	Guess 2	Guess 3

Guessing and Checking

1. I am thinking of two numbers. When I add them the total is 14.
    When I multiply these numbers the answer is greater than 40 but less than 50.
    What numbers are they?

	1st guess	2nd guess	3rd guess	4th guess	5th guess
1st number					
2nd number					
Added =					
Multiplied =					
✓ = right X = wrong					

Sometimes there can be more than one correct answer to a problem. When you've found one correct answer, continue checking for others.

In this problem there are _____ correct combinations:

_____ and _____ = _____, _____ × _____ = _____ which is correct.

_____ and _____ = _____, _____ × _____ = _____ which is correct also.

_____ and _____ = _____, _____ × _____ = _____ which is correct also.

Let's try out another problem like the one above.

2. When I add the two numbers the total is 9. When I multiply the numbers the answer is more than a dozen. Find the numbers to answer this.

	1st guess	2nd guess	3rd guess	4th guess	5th guess
1st number					
2nd number					
Added =					
Multiplied =					
✓ = right X = wrong					

Activities

1. Karen was born in a month which ends with the letter R. This month's name has a total of 7 letters. In which month was she born?

Step 1: List all the months of the year which end with the letter R.

_____

Step 2: Count the number of letters in each name.

Answer: Karen was born in_____ .

2. Kay has a pile of coins (all equal or less than one dollar). Show how she can make stacks of coins equal to one dollar. Some combinations are obvious – one 1 dollar coin. For other combinations you will need to guess and check. Show at least 10 different combinations of coins.

3. There were bicycles and tricycles in the back yard. I counted a total of 13 wheels on 5 vehicles. How many of each were in the back yard?

1st guess	2nd guess	3rd guess
_____ bicycles	_____ bicycles	_____ bicycles
_____ tricycles	_____ tricycles	_____ tricycles
_____ wheels	_____ wheels	_____ wheels

4. I counted a total of 10 motor cars and motorcycles. There were 34 wheels on the ground. How many of each were parked there?

1st guess	2nd guess	3rd guess
_____ cars	_____ cars	_____ cars
_____ motorcycles	_____ motorcycles	_____ motorcycles
_____ wheels	_____ wheels	_____ wheels

Guessing and Checking

1. The total age of Marcia and her father is 38 years. When you take Marcia's age from her father's age, the difference is a score of 20 years. How old are Marcia and her father?

One important fact is needed before you can begin solving this problem: "What is the value of one score?"

Now we know that, let's get to the facts: Marcia + Dad = _____ years.

Dad - Marcia = _____ years.

Let's set up a table so that we can record our guesses and checks.

	1st guess	2nd guess	3rd guess	4th guess	5th guess
Dad's age	32				
Marcia's age	6				
Added	38				
Subtracted					
Check: ✓ or ✗					

In the first guess I chose 32 and 6. When added, the total is 38.

This is correct. 32 - 6 = _____. This is correct / not correct, so my guess is right / wrong. Fill in the table.

2. A jar of jam costs 72 cents to produce.
   The cost of the jam is three times more than the cost of the jar and lid.
   Find the cost of the contents and the cost of the jar and lid.

Let's put this information into the form of a diagram.

cost of jar + lid × _____   =   cost of jam

Set up this table to help you guess and check to find the answer.

Cost of					
Multiplied by					
Cost of					
Total cost					
Check: ✓ or ✗					

Activities

1. This number has two digits. When the digits are added the total is 9.
When the two digits are taken away from each other the difference is 3.
This number is bigger than 50 but less than 100. What is the number?

	1st guess	2nd guess			
1st digit					
2nd digit					
Added					
Subtracted					
> 50 > 100					
Check: ✓ or ✗					

2. This number is greater than 20 but less than 50. When the two digits are
added the total is 9. When the digits are multiplied the answer is a score.
(Do you remember the value of one score?) Here is a grid for you to work on.
Fill in all the details.

3. Use only 'gold' coins in any combination to make up $10.
Draw all of your combinations. Don't forget to check your combinations.

**How much did you learn?
Try the test on page 31.**

Working Backwards

1. If I take 18 from a number then add 6 and the answer is 12, what was the original number? Let's look at this as a diagram.

original number	take away 18	add 6		answer 12
			=	

We could guess numbers and check to see if they are right OR we could work backwards. Let's try that.

☆ The answer is 12.

☆ To get this answer, 6 was added so the number must have been _____.

☆ What number would I need to take 18 from to get my answer of 6 _____.
   (Hint: add 6 and 18 to achieve this.)

☆ Let's now check.   ☆ Take 18 from your answer = _____.

☆ Now add 6 = _____.   ☆ This answer should be 12. Is it?   Yes / No

2. I thought of a number then added 5. Then I subtracted 7. My answer is 21. What was the number I first thought of?

original number	add	take away		answer
			=	

☆ Now start working backwards.

☆ The final answer was _____.

☆ To get that answer I took 7 from _____ to get 21.

☆ To find my first number I added 5 to _____ to get 28.

☆ My original number was _____.

Here is one for you to try by yourself.

3. To the original number I added 6 then took away 9. The result was 14. With which number did I start?

original number	add	take away		answer
			=	

_____

_____

Activities

1. From her purse, Gina spent $8 on a magazine and lollies.
   Her dad then gave her $10 pocket money. Gina now has $13.
   How much did Gina have before her spending spree?

☆ Draw your diagram

| | | | = | |

☆ Now work backwards.

_____

_____

_____

_____

☆ Don't forget to check your answer.

2. There was some flour in the canister. Mum used 2 kg making scones.
   When she went shopping, Mum bought 4 kg of flour which she added to the canister. The canister now has 5 kg of flour in it.
   How much flour was in the canister before Mum made the scones?

| | | | = | |

☆ Now work backwards.

_____

_____

_____

_____

☆ Enter your answer into the problem and check to make sure you are right.

Working Backwards

1. I doubled my money by doing odd jobs for Mrs Smith. I spent $5 on blank videos. This left me with $13. This means I must have had $_____ before I started the odd jobs.

This problem involves doubling (multiplying) and subtraction. The method is the same but the processes have changed. Let's draw a diagram.

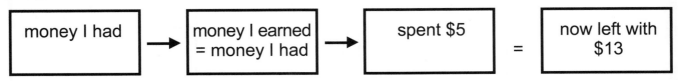

| money I had | → | money I earned = money I had | → | spent $5 | = | now left with $13 |

☆ If I spent $5 and had $13 left, I must have had $_____.

☆ The money I had equals the money I earned; the total of that is $18.

Earnings must equal $_____ and money I had must equal $_____ too.

☆ Enter the answer into your problem. Work forwards to check.

You work this one, following the steps provided.

2. Poi's pet calf doubled its mass by the end of last month. Unfortunately, it got sick and lost 15 kg. The vet weighed the calf and found it now weighed 85 kg. Work out how much the calf weighed at the beginning of last month.

☆ Fill in the missing details in the diagram.

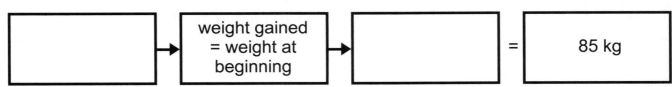

| | → | weight gained = weight at beginning | → | | = | 85 kg |

☆ The calf lost _____ kg and ended up weighing 85 kg, so its mass before it

got sick must have been _____ kg.

☆ Its mass at the beginning of the month equalled the gain in mass that month.

Therefore, the two equal numbers which total 100 kg must be _____ kg and

_____ kg.

☆ The answer is _____ kg.

You must always check. Enter the answer into the problem and work forwards.

Is your answer correct / incorrect?

Activities

Try these yourself. Remember the steps.

☆ READ the problem.
☆ DRAW a flow diagram to make it easier to understand.
☆ SOLVE the problem.
☆ CHECK your answer by working forwards.

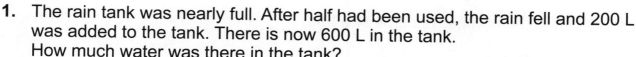

1. The rain tank was nearly full. After half had been used, the rain fell and 200 L was added to the tank. There is now 600 L in the tank.
    How much water was there in the tank?

☆ Diagram

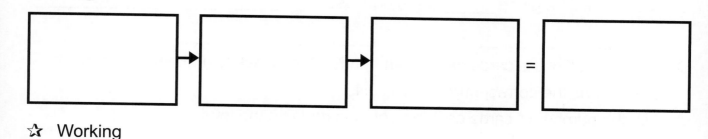

☆ Working

_____

_____

_____

☆ Did you check your answer? Was it right / wrong?

2. Bill had some marbles in his bag. He gave half to Mike, then won 15 from Tim. When he counted, his total was 25. How many did he start with?

☆ Diagram

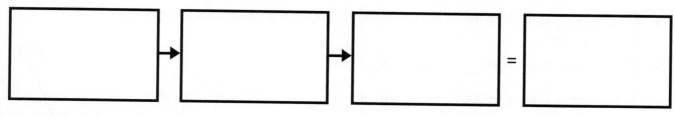

☆ Working

_____

_____

_____

☆ Check your answer by working forwards.

Acting It Out

1. A group of children have sporting hero cards. Seung has 3. Marla has 2 more than Seung. Jordan has double the number that Marla owns and Cassie has six less than Jordan. How many cards do the children have among them?

☆ Use a labelled mug for each person and cut up pieces of paper for the cards.

☆ Give 'Seung' the number of cards he should have: _____.

☆ Hand 'Marla' the number of cards she has: _____ + _____ = _____.

☆ Count out 'Jordan's' _____ cards.

☆ 'Cassie' will be given _____ cards because _____

_____

☆ Now that all of the cards have been handed out, check to make sure that each

person has the correct number. Yes / No

☆ List the number of cards each person has and find the total.

☆ Check this by gathering up the cards and counting them.

☆ Write your answers here:

SEUNG _____ cards + MARLA _____ cards + JORDAN _____ cards +

CASSIE _____ cards = _____ cards.

2. There are 6 people in a line in the supermarket. Each person has double the number of grocery items as the person in front of them. If the first person has only one item, how many items do all the customers buy?

☆ Use _____ containers for the people and blocks/counters to represent grocery items.

☆ The first person has _____ item(s).

☆ The second person has _____ items.

☆ Person 3 has _____.

☆ _____ items were bought by the fourth person.

☆ Number 5 in line has _____ items.

☆ The last in line has _____ items.

☆ Find the total. _____

☆ Check your working throughout the problem.

Activities

1. There are four people in my family - Mum, Dad, Tony and me. At Christmas time we all give each other a present. How many presents are exchanged?

   ☆ You will need _____ toys to represent people and blocks/counters as presents.

   ☆ Mum gives _____ presents.

   ☆ _____ presents are given by Dad.

   ☆ Tony hands out _____ presents.

   ☆ I need _____ presents.

   ☆ Check to make sure that everyone gets presents.

   ☆ Find the total number of presents. _____

   ☆ Check your working by collecting up the 'presents' from the people and finding the total. My answer is right / wrong.

2. When the Cardell family (Mr Cardell, Mrs Cardell, Gina and Brett) went overseas, Brett carried the lightest suitcase (only 5 kg). Gina's suitcase was 3 kg heavier than Brett's. Mrs Cardell always takes a lot. Her suitcase was double the mass of Gina's, but Mr Cardell had the heaviest. It was 3 kg heavier than Mrs Cardell's. Find the total mass of all of the suitcases.

   ☆ Use boxes to represent the suitcases.

   ☆ How heavy was Brett's? _____ kg. Mark this on the first box under Brett's name.

   ☆ Work out the mass Gina carried. _____ kg. Record this mass under Gina's name on the second box.

   ☆ Repeat this process for Mrs Cardell's suitcase which weighed _____ kg.

   ☆ Repeat the process to find the mass of Mr Cardell's suitcase. _____ kg

   ☆ Record the masses of the suitcases here after checking your working.

Brett	Gina	Mrs Cardell	Mr Cardell
kg	kg	kg	kg

   ☆ Now find the total: _____ kg.

   ☆ Add the numbers in a different order, e.g. backwards, to make sure that your total is correct.

Acting It Out

1. How many red roses will the florist have to provide to this wedding party?
There's the bride, 3 bridesmaids, a flower girl, the groom and 2 groom's men.
The bride will carry a bunch of a dozen roses.
Each bridesmaid will have a bunch of half a dozen and the flower girl will carry 3.
The groom and groom's men will each have a red rose in their coat lapel.

☆ Complete the table with the people's names and the number of roses each will have. Check the problem to make sure that you have the right numbers.

Bride	Brides-maid 1						

☆ Now find the total: _____.

☆ Check your total. My answer is   right / wrong.

2. 100 children had to cast their vote for school captain. The votes were collected in 4 boxes. In the first box a score of votes was counted. In the second box there were six more votes than in the first box. The total in the third box was half of box 2. The fourth box had double the number of the first box. Did all the children vote? (Note: a *score* is a term meaning 'twenty'.)

☆ Gather 4 boxes and 100 counters to represent the 'votes'.
Label the boxes 1 to 4.

☆ Box 1 has _____ votes. Put that number of counters in this box.

☆ Box 2 has _____ votes. Count the number of votes into this box.

☆ _____ votes were in Box 3. Add that number to the box.

☆ There were _____ votes in Box 4. Put those votes in the box.

☆ Check your working from the problem.

☆ Do you have any counters (votes) left over?   Yes / No

☆ Total up the number of votes to make sure that you haven't miscounted.

☆ Did all the children vote?   Yes / No

☆ How many children didn't vote in the election? _____

Year 3: Unit 5
Activities

1. At the train station I saw:
☆ an elderly man with two suitcases.
☆ a man with an umbrella and a briefcase.
☆ two travellers each with 3 pieces of luggage.
☆ a porter with a dozen bags on his trolley.
☆ four school children each carrying their school bags.
☆ five young travellers each with a big backpack.

How many pieces of luggage were seen? _____

You will need _____ toys to represent people. Use counters/blocks for the luggage.

☆ Don't forget to check your working and your total.

2. I have 60 jelly beans and 6 jars. In the first jar I put 1 lolly.
Two were put in the second jar. The third jar had 4 put in it.
In the next jar, double that number were added.
The same (double the previous) were added to the next jar.
Will there be enough jelly beans to double the number for the sixth jar? Yes / No

If not, how many short will I be? _____

Use cups or jars, and counters for the jelly beans. Check your working.

3. At the pet show there were 5 displays – dogs, cats, birds, mice and fish.
I counted a dozen dogs and a score of cats.
There were 6 more birds than the total number of cats and dogs.
The total number of mice was 10 less than the birds, but the total number of fish was 10 more than the mice.

In all, there were _____ animals.

Dogs	
Cats	
Birds	
Mice	
Fish	
Total	

☆ Use 5 containers to represent the displays.
☆ Use counters/blocks to represent animals.
☆ Count out the number for the dogs.
☆ Add the correct number of counters/blocks to represent the cats.
☆ Repeat this process for the birds, the mice and the fish.
☆ Find your total.
☆ What did the question ask? _____
☆ Did you answer the question? Yes / No. Did you check your calculations?

How much did you learn?
Try the test on page 32.

Creating a Table

A table is a much clearer way of representing information than a great number of words.

Buses leave our stop on the hour every hour between 9 a.m. and 5 p.m. every Monday. On Tuesday, our hourly service starts at 10 a.m. and the last bus is at 4 p.m. Wednesday is the same as Tuesday. On Thursday, the buses start at 9 a.m. and end at 8 p.m. Friday start time is 10 a.m. and the last bus is at 7 p.m. On Saturdays and Sundays the first bus is at 10 a.m. and then every two hours till 6 p.m.

	9 a.m	10 a.m.	11 a.m.	noon								
Monday	✓	✓	✓	✓	✓	✓	✓	✓	✓			
Tuesday												

☆ Finish entering the days of the week in the first column.

☆ Times are written across the top row. Complete this row.

☆ The ticks for Monday indicate the times buses leave. Check they are correct.

If a space is not ticked it means that no bus leaves.

☆ Enter the information for Tuesday.

☆ Carefully read the information for the times of the other days.
Enter the information one day at a time.

☆ Check your work to make sure your table agrees with the information given.

I'm sure you'll agree a table is much easier to understand than a paragraph of words.

Activities

PETE'S PET PLACE

SALE	
Comets	$1.50
Shubunkins	$2.00
Orandas	$1.60
Pearl Scales	$2.50
Bubble Eyes	$3.00

1. Use this advertisement to work out the cost of:

   a) 4 Shubunkins _____

   b) 3 Orandas _____

   c) 6 Comets _____

   d) 2 Bubble Eyes _____

   e) 4 Pearl Scales _____

2. Caitlin purchased 3 Comets, 2 Orandas and a Bubble Eye.

   If she handed over $20, how much change should she receive? _____

3. Len likes Comets. How many could he buy for $10? _____

   What change, if any, would he receive? _____

4. Convert the following into a table.

Rick's Restaurant is closed on Monday and Tuesday. On Wednesday, Rick's opens at 5 p.m. and closes at 9 p.m. Thursday is late night shopping, so Rick's opens at 5 p.m. and closes at 10 p.m. On Friday, the restaurant is open between 7 p.m. and midnight. On Saturday, it opens from 12 noon till 2 p.m. for lunch and 5 p.m. to midnight for dinner. On Sunday, the hours are 12 noon to 2 p.m. for lunch and 5 p.m. to 9 p.m. for dinner.

	12 p.m.													
Monday & Tuesday														

☆ Enter the days down the first column.
☆ Enter the times - earliest to latest - across the top row.
☆ Use colours to show when Rick's is open.

Creating a List

Making a list can help you find all of the combinations.
Follow this example.

At the local delicatessen you can buy sandwiches with two fillings for $2.50.
The choice of fillings is tomato, ham, egg, lettuce, onion.

☆ How many different types of sandwiches can be made?

☆ Write down the fillings.
Start with the first two items: _____ and _____ .

☆ For the second type, still use tomato but add the next item, _____ .
This makes a second type of sandwich.

☆ Let's record this in a list.

Tomato and ham			
Tomato and _____			
Tomato and _____			
Tomato and _____			

☆ The second group is made by taking the second and third items, the second and fourth, then the second and fifth. Enter these in the second group.

Note: Ham and tomato is the same as tomato and ham so it can't be included in the second list.

☆ The third group is formed with the third and fourth items and the third and fifth items.

Why can't you have egg and tomato/egg and ham?

☆ The fourth group is a mix of items four and five.

Why is there only one item in the last group?

☆ Now count up the number of combinations. _____

☆ Check to make sure that you have included each combination only once (e.g. egg and lettuce is the same as lettuce and egg.)

The local delicatessen can make _____ different types of sandwiches using 5 different fillings.

Activities

1. Mary has red, white and blue socks. She has brown and black shoes.
    How many different combinations can she wear?

Use a logical approach. Make a list. Check each combination, one at a time.

Black shoes with	Brown shoes with
○	○
○	○
○	○

☆ Count up the combinations. _____

☆ Check to make sure that you haven't left out a combination or written the same combination twice.

2. Jacquie has 3 skirts (red, green and black) and 4 blouses (white, cream, navy and striped). How many different outfits can she create with these?

Take the skirts one at a time, then add a different blouse to make a different outfit.

○	○	○
○	○	○
○	○	○
○	○	○

☆ Total number of different outfits = _____ Check your combinations.

3. How many different 3-digit numbers can you make with these digits – 3, 4, 5?

Those that begin with 3	Those that begin with _____	Those that begin with _____

☆ Count up the numbers. _____ Check your combinations.

How much did you learn?
Try the test on page 33.

Test 1

Finding a Pattern and Drawing a Picture

Let's see how well you can solve these problems using either Finding a Pattern or Drawing a Picture.

1. Complete the missing parts here.

    a) △, △△, △, △△, △, , , .

    b) 55, 65, 75, 85, _____, _____, _____.

    c) ⊘, ⊕, ⊛, , , .

    d) (dot patterns), , , , .

    e) $2.20, $3.20, $4.20, $5.20, _____, _____, _____.

2. Six people were each carrying 3 bottles of drink. One person dropped 2 and these broke. How many bottles remain?

    Show working here.

3. At Swimming Club last week here's how Talia, Sam, Marg, Ian and Tye finished the 100 m freestyle. Marg did not finish in front of the other 4. Tye was 1 m in front of Marg. Talia was 3 metres in front of Tye and 1 m in front of Ian. Sam was 2 metres in front of Ian.
    Write down the finishing order from first to fifth.

    Working space.

4. Show at least 5 ways of giving 90 cents change using a range of coins.

a)	b)	c)	d)	e)

Guessing and Checking

Use the strategy of guessing and checking to solve these.

Problem	Working Space	Answer
1. If I add 2 digits, the answer is 11. If I multiply these 2 digits, my answer is 30. Name the 2 digits.		
2. Jack caught 32 fish. He counted 10 more whiting than bream. How many whiting did he catch?		
3. I have some 50 cent coins. I have double that number of 20 cent coins. Altogether I have $4.50. How many of each coin do I have?		
4. In the paddock I counted legs - 36. I counted heads - 10. If there were people and cattle in the paddock, how many people were working the cattle?		
5. Grandma is 52 years older than young Tom. When you add Tom's age to his grandma's age, the total is 68 years. How old are each of these people?		
6. On the table were spiders and ants. Tina said that she counted only 6 bodies. Mike was quick. He counted a total of 40 legs. Gina said that she didn't need to look. She knew there were _____ ants and _____ spiders on the table.		

Test 3

Working Backwards and Acting It Out

Solve these by either Working Backwards or Acting It Out.

1. Find the missing number. I added 8 then doubled the result to get an answer of 20. What is the missing number?

    ☆ What strategy will you use? _____

    ☆ Describe how you solved this problem. _____

    _____

    ☆ My answer is _____.

    ☆ Show how you checked your answer. _____

    _____

2. Last Christmas, Leena received 3 more presents than Skye. Skye was given 2 less presents than Paul. If Paul was given 8 presents, how many did Leena receive?

    ☆ How will you solve this? _____

    _____

    Show working here.

    ☆ Leena received _____ presents. Prove you are right by checking.

3. In the Cartwright family (Mum, Dad, Sean, Gloria and baby Valerie), everyone gave a present to each of the other members of the family (except Valerie, who is too young to give presents, but can still receive them). How many presents did the members of the Cartwright family purchase?

    ☆ I will solve this by_____

    _____

    Here is my working.

    ☆ The answer is _____ presents. Prove you are right by checking.

Answers
Year 3

Page 3
1a) 2 birds   b) top hat   c) 3 footballs

2a) b) c) d) e)

Page 4
1. 16, 32
2. 66, 56

Page 5
1a)   b) 2 sheep,   3 sheep   c)

d)

2a) 10, 12, 14, 16, 18
b) 2, 7, 1, 7, 0
c) 300, 350, 400, 450, 500
d) 500, 400, 300, 200, 100

3a) 5, 6
b) 50 c, 60 c, 70 c, 80 c

c)

Page 6
1c) (i) one   (ii) 4   (iii) Tom, Mary
(iv) more   (v) 1, 4, 2, 5
2c) 7   d) 14

Page 7
1a) 7 L   b) 10 chairs
c) Mary, Jill, Tom, Scott
d)

are just some ways.

e) 3 trips

Page 8
1. Vanessa, Carly, Mike;   Carly, Mike, Vanessa; Carly, Vanessa, Mike - 6 ways.
2. 10, 20, \$1, 50;   10, 50, 20 \$1;
   20, 10, \$1, 50;   20, \$1, 50; 10;
   20, \$1, 10, 50;   50, 20, 10 \$1;
   50, 10, 20, \$1;   50, \$1, 10, 20;
   50, \$1, 20, 10;   \$1, 50, 20, 10;
   \$1, 20, 50, 10;   \$1, 20, 10, 50;
   \$1, 10, 50, 20;   \$1, 10, 20, 50

Page 9
1. The cross can be red/white/blue; the background red/white/blue; the stars red/white/blue
2. GYG; GGY; GGG; YYY; YYG;
3. GGGG; GYGG; GGYG; GGGY; GGYY; GYGY; GYYG; GYYY; YGYY; YYGY; YYYG; YYYY

Page 10
1c) 1 d) Anna, Chris, Barry, David
2. There are many combinations.

Page 11
1. 14 m   2. 7 posts
3. 11 taxis   4. 4 trips
5. 7 times

Page 12
1. 2 x 20 c   3 x 10 c
2. 543   3. 12 boys, 17 girls

Page 13
1. 15 cattle, 23 sheep
2. 4 x \$1, 8 x 50 c
3. 5 x \$1 and 10 x 50 c

Page 14
1. 9 and 5, or 8 and 6, or 7 and 7
2. 7 and 2, 6 and 3, 5 and 4

Page 15
1. October
2. 2 x 50c; 1 x 50 c + 2 x 20 c + 1 x 10 c;
   1 x 50 c + 1 x 20 c + 3 x 10 c;
   1 x 50 c + 5 x 10 c; 5 x 20 c;
   4 x 20 c + 2 x 10 c; 3 x 20 c + 4 x 10 c;
   2 x 20c + 6 x 10 c; 1 x 20 c + 8 x 10 c;
   10 x 10 c plus other combinations using 5 c coins, e.g. 1 x 50 c + 2 x 20 c + 2 x 5 c... to 20 x 5 c
3. 2 bicycles, 3 tricycles
4. 7 cars, 3 motor cycles

Page 16
1. Dad 29, Marcia 9
2. 18 cents jar and lid, 54 c contents

Page 17
1. 63   2. 45
3. 5 x \$2; 4 x \$2 + 2 x \$1; 3 x \$2 + 4 x \$1; 2 x \$2 + 6 x \$1; 1 x \$2 + 8 x \$1; 10 x \$1

Page 18
1. 24   2. 23
3. 17

Page 19
1. \$11   2. 3 kg

Page 20
1. \$9; \$18, \$9, \$9
2. 50 kg; 15 kg, 100 kg, 50 kg, 50 kg

Page 21
1. 800 L   2. 20 marbles

Page 22
1. 3, 5, 10, 4, total 22
2. 1, 2, 4, 8, 16, 32 = 63

Page 23
1. 3, 3, 3, 3 = 12
2. 5 kg, 8 kg, 16 kg, 19 kg = 48 kg

Page 24
1. Bride 12, bridesmaids 18, flower girl 3, groom/groomsmen 3   total: 36 roses
2. No - I didn't; 1 - 20, 2 - 26, 3 - 13, 4 - 40

Answers cont.

Page 25
1. 31 pieces of luggage; 14
2. No, 3 short   3. 136 animals

Page 26
Mon - 9 am, 10 am, 11 am, noon, 1 pm, 2 pm,
    3 pm, 4 pm, 5 pm
Tue - 10 am, 11 am, noon, 1 pm, 2 pm, 3 pm, 4 pm
Wed - 10 am, 11 am, noon, 1 pm, 2 pm, 3 pm, 4 pm
Thur - 9 am, 10 am, 11 am, noon, 1 pm, 2 pm,
    3 pm, 4 pm, 5 pm, 6 pm, 7 pm, 8 pm
Fri - 10 am, 11 am, noon, 1 pm, 2 pm, 3 pm,
    4 pm, 5 pm, 6 pm, 7 pm
Sat - 10 am, noon, 2 pm, 4 pm, 6 pm
Sun - 10 am, noon, 2 pm, 4 pm, 6 pm

Page 27
1a) $8   b) $4.80   c) $9.00
d) $6.00   e) $10.00
2. $9.30   3. 6 with $1.00 change
4. Parent/teacher to check:
Mon & Tue: closed; Wed: 5 pm - 9 pm;
Thur: 5 pm - 10 pm; Fri: 7 pm - 12 am;
Sat: noon - 2 pm, 5 pm - 12 am;
Sun: noon - 2 pm, 5 pm - 9 pm

Page 28
tomato & ham, tomato & egg, tomato & lettuce,
tomato & onion;
ham & egg, ham & lettuce, ham & onion;
egg & lettuce, egg & onion;
lettuce & onion
10 combinations

Page 29
1

Black shoes with	Brown shoes with
○ red ○ white ⟩socks ○ blue	○ red ○ white ⟩socks ○ blue

1a) 6 combinations   2. 12 outfits
3. 6 numbers (345, 354, 435, 453, 534, 543)

Test 1 - Page 30
1a)

b) 95, 105, 115
c)

d) • • • •
      • • • • • •
    • • • •

e) $6.20, $7.20, $8.20
2. 16
3. Sam, Talia, Ian, Tye, Marg
4. 50 c + 2 x 20 c, 50 c + 20 c + 2 x 10 c,
    50 c + 4 x 10 c, 4 x 20 c + 1 x 10 c,
    3 x 20 c + 3 x 10 c, 2 x 20 c + 5 x 10 c,
    20 c + 7 x 10 c, 9 x 10 c, other
    combinations using 5 cent coins

Test 2 - Page 31
1. 5 and 6   2. 21 whiting
3. 10 twenty cent coins and 5 fifty cent coins
4. 2 people   5. 60 and 8
6. 2 spiders, 4 ants

Test 3 - Page 32
1. 2   2. 9 presents
3. 16 presents

Test 4 - Page 33
1. 8 burgers
2. 4 numbers: 516, 561, 615, 651
3.

kg	1	2	3	4	5	6	7	8
Cost	$2	$4	$6	$8	$10	$12	$14	$16

4. apple and orange, apple and pineapple,
apple and apricot, apple and lemon,
orange and pineapple, orange and apricot,
orange and lemon, pineapple and apricot,
pineapple and lemon, apricot and lemon
(12 flavours)

Page 34
a) circle   b) circle
c) 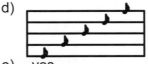   d)
e) circle, 8   f) 11
g) 11th

Year 4
Page 35
1a) staff, bars   b) notes
c) going up 1 line each time then repeating
d)

e) yes
2a) tree   b) apples
c) number increasing by 1
d) 5 apples, 6 apples, 7 apples, 1 tree

Page 36
1a) multiples of/counting in 5s
b) decreasing by 5s c) 15, 10, 5, 0
d) decreasing in 5s
2a) even   b) increasing
c) 30, 32, 34, 36, 38, 40
d) increasing, even
3a) multiples of/counting in 11s
b) decreasing c) 55, 44, 33, 22
4a) 5   b) 7
c) 9   d) 11
e) 5, 7, 9, 11   f) yes
g) yes   h) correct
i) 13, 15, 17, 19, 21

Page 37

1. number of sides increasing, 4 sides, 5 sides, 6 sides
2. counting up in 3s: 24, 27, 30
3. counting back in 30s: 440, 410, 380
4. increasing number of sections (parts) coloured: 5, 6, 7 parts coloured
5. increasing number of sloping lines: 5, 6, 7 lines
6. increasing (by 2) ordinal numbers: sixteenth, eighteenth, twentieth
7. decreasing (by 1) number of pencils: 4, 3, 2 pencils
8. counting up in thousands: 4001, 5001, 6001
9. counting back from $1 in ten cents: 70 c, 60 c, 50 c
10. increasing (by 5 kg) masses: 50 kg, 55 kg, 60 kg

Page 38

1a) red, green, blue   b) green, blue, red
c) green, red, blue
2. many combinations - check

Page 39

a) 12, 9, 20, 15, 11, 11
b) total number of books
c) by adding   d) 78
e) true
f) 3, 2, more, yes - possibly bigger books, 63

Page 40

1a) False   b) False
c) 17   d) more
e) 8
2. There are 24 possible combinations.

Page 41

1b) 100 L   c) ½
d) 50 L   e) 15 L
f) 35 L
2b) 1 kg   c) 2 kg
d) 4 kg, 8 kg, 16 kg, 32 kg
e) 4 kg, 5, 32 kg, 128 kg

Page 42

1. 50 c; 2 x 20 c + 10 c; 1 x 20 c + 3 x 10 c; 5 x 10 c; 10 x 5 c
   No - there are 20 combinations
2a) 45 m   b) 2, 4, 3, 6
c) add all the lengths sold then subtract, or subtract each length from 45
d) 30 m
3b) (i) 2 (ii) 8 (iii) 24 (iv) 72

Page 43

1. 250 cm   2. 15 posts
3. check drawings for each window = 12 possibilities

Page 44

1a) 12   b) 8 x 3 legs + 4 x 4 legs

Page 45

1a) 54; 15 chickens, 6 guinea pigs
2. 20 chickens, 1 guinea pig

Page 46

1a) 21, Yes, 9, No   b) 21, Yes, 5, Yes
c) 9 and 12, 21, Yes, 3, Yes
2. 18 and 35

Page 47

a) cheeseburger and sundae
b) burger, large chips, ice-cream
c) cheeseburger, small drink, regular chips, sundae

Page 48

1. 8 cars and 3 trucks
2a) Tran $1.90, me $1.30, Li $1.20
b) Tran $2, me $1.40, Li $1.30

Page 49

1. 12 kangaroos, 6 wombats
2. 36 and 63

Page 50

1a) $65   b) $20
c) $45   d) $40
e) add $45 and $40   f) $85
2a) 6°C   b) 8°C
c) 14°C   d) 12°C
e) subtract   f) 2°C

Page 51

1. ended with 95, gained 19, so had 76, gave away 36, so originally has 112; 12 more than a hundred. Prove by working forwards.
2. ended with 9000, gained 5000 so had 4000, lost 3000, so won 7000 on first ball. Work forwards.

Page 52

1a) 11   b) 5 less   c) 6
d) 3 more   e) 9   f) 26, correct
2a) 26   b) 9 more   c) 35
d) 4 more   e) 39   f) 39, 35, 26
g) worked forwards

Page 53

1a) work backwards
b) chimps = 18 + 13 = 21, monkeys = 11 + 21 = 32, apes = 8
c) total 61 animals
d) check back into problem and work forwards
2a) Start with Gloria. Find Val's then Harvey's score.
b) G = 32, V = 32 + 26 = 58, H = 58 - 16 = 42
   Order = Val 58, Harvey 42, Gloria 32

Page 54

1a) No - not more than 10 coins
b) 11 coins, Yes   c) No   d) 16
e) 3 stacks + 1   f) Yes   g) 16 coins
h) No - $20   i) 16 coins   j) $16
2. 36 coins = $36

Page 55

1. Harry, Henry, Hans, Herbert
2a) 10   b) 2   c) 10
d) 2   e) 10   f) 2
g) No   h) 10   i) Yes
j) 46 minutes

Answers cont.

Page 56

1a) you + 6 = 7
b) 7 + 3 = 10
c) 10 - 1 = 9
d) 9 + 4 = 13
e) 13 - 1 = 12
f) 12 + 2 = 14 - 5 = 9
g) 3 on 3 off = 9 on the bus
2a) 32
b) 1st station 32 + 10 - 5 = 37
c) 2nd station 37 + 6 - 8 = 35
d) 3rd station 35 + 16 - 3 = 48
e) 4th station 48 + 4 - 10 = 42
f) 42 people on train at end
g) work problem backwards to end up with 32
h) 42

Page 57

1a) using counters act it out
b) Must have 31 - 39 coins. Try each one till combination is found. Check for other combinations which work.
c) $3.20
d) try other combinations
2. Maria, oldest, bank manager; Guiseppi, middle, mechanic; Carlo, youngest, plasterer
3. Rupert, Kerry, John, Rose

Page 58

1a) 1735, 1753
b) 3571, 3715, 3751
c) 5137, 5173, 5317, 5371, 5713, 5137
d) 7135, 7153, 7315, 7351, 7513, 7531
e) check table
f) 7513
g) 3157, 3175
h) 5731, 5713, 5371, 5317, 5173, 5137

Page 59

1a) 8, 9, 10; 12, 48, 60, 84, 96, 108, 120
b) 60, 8, 10 dozen, 5, 4
2. Table: 3, 6, 9, 11, 12, 13; $16, $32, $64, $128, $256, $512, $1024, $2048, $4096, $8192
a) $64
b) 10th
c) $127
d) $8192
e) $16 383
f) no

Page 60

c) black
e) navy
f) red, black, black
h) navy
i) red, blue, black
j) red, red, tan
k) red, red, navy
l) red, red, black
m) 12
n) white grey tan, white grey navy, white grey black, white black tan, white black navy, white black black, white blue tan, white blue navy, white blue black, white red tan, white red navy, white red black
o) 12 p) 12 q) 12 r) 12 s) 36

Page 61

1. 12 different meals
2a) baker - bread, pies, birthday cake; butcher - mince, steak, sausages, dog bones; hairdresser - trim; supermarket - butter, sugar, soft drink, milk, detergent, flour, peanuts
b) hairdresser - unhealthy to have food there supermarket - furthest from home; butcher - next on the way home, heavy; baker - closest to home, delicate cake

Test 1 - Page 62

1a) 42, 35, 28, 21
b)

c) 52, 54, 56, 58
d) 505, 606, 707, 808
2. rwb, rbw, wbr, wrb, brw, bwr - 6 combinations
3a) check drawing
b) take 10 from 50 then halve
c) 20 kg
4. check drawing – 6 ways

Test 2 - Page 63

1. 20 bicycles, 2 unicycles
2. 7 oranges, 8 apples
3. 22 and 59

Test 3 - Page 64

1. Marie, Gail, Ross, John
2. 89 kg
3. Take $15 off $50 to find how much I had after spending $20. Add $20 to this amount to find original amount of money.
4a) acting it out
b) arrange people, check arrangement, rearrange if necessary
c) Phil first, Jill second, Bill third, Lill last
d) check problem against answer - should all be true
5. 58

Test 4 - Page 65

1. check listing for 9 sandwiches
white + ham/chicken/lamb (3)
brown + ham/chicken/lamb (3)
wholemeal + ham/chicken/lamb (3)
2a) $1.50, $3, $4.50, $6, $7.50, $9, $10.50, $12, $13.50, $15, $16.50
b) 4 kg
c) $10.50
d) No - $13.50
e) 10 kg = $15, 20 kg = $30
3a) 15 days
b) V&S, V&C, V&K, V&R, V&M, S&C, S&K, S&R, S&M, C&K, C&M, C&V, K&R, K&M, R&M

Creating a list or a table will help you solve these.

1. In the take-away you can have either beef patties, steak, fish or chicken with salad on your burger. You can choose to have onion or no onion.

   If I want one of every possible combination, I will have to order _____ burgers.

Show your working here.

   ☆ My order will be for _____ burgers.

   ☆ I checked my working by _____

   _____

2. Create as many three digit numbers greater than 500 as you can using these digits: 6, 5 and 1.

   ☆ Here are all the numbers I *could* make: _____

   _____

   ☆ I must remove _____ and _____ because _____

   _____

   ☆ This leaves me with _____ numbers: _____, _____, _____, _____.

3. Complete this table showing the cost of mince per kilogram.

Number of kg	1	2	3	4	5	6		
Cost		$4						

4. Make lists of all the different flavours you could create using the juice from any two of these fruit: apple, orange, pineapple, apricot and lemon.

Finding a Pattern

Patterns are to be found all around us. Check out these patterns as we work together.

Here is a geometric pattern.

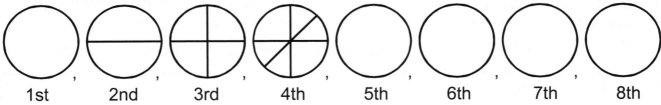

1st , 2nd , 3rd , 4th , 5th , 6th , 7th , 8th

☆ The first circle has no diameters drawn in.

☆ The second circle has 1 diameter.

☆ The third has 2 diameters drawn in.

☆ The fourth circle has 3 diameters shown.

Let's look at what is and is not changing.

☆ In each case, the unchanging element is a circle.

☆ What is changing is the number of diameters.

☆ Here's how this part is changing: 0, 1, 2, 3...

☆ To be a pattern, this increase must continue at the same rate. So the next

   element should be (a) a _____ with _____ diameters followed by (b) a

   _____ with _____ diameters drawn in, and so on.

Complete the next four elements in this series.

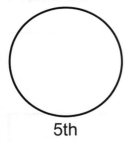 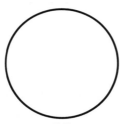 (c) 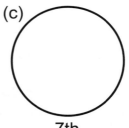 (d)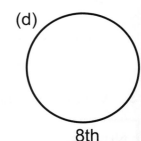

5th   6th   7th   8th

To solve and find patterns:

   ☆ Look for what is and is not changing.

   ☆ Ask: How are the changes taking place? (increasing/decreasing)

   ☆ Predict the next elements.

   ☆ Check your work to make sure your elements fit the pattern.

The ninth element is (e) a _____ with _____ diameters, the 12th element has

(f) _____ diameters drawn in a circle, while a circle with 10 diameters drawn in

   is the (g) _____ element of this series.

Activities

Here is a musical pattern.

1.

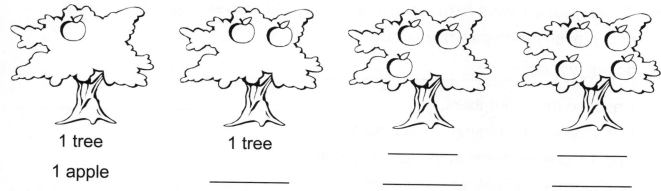

a) What is the same? staff, bars, notes (circle your choice[s]).

b) What is changing? staff, notes, bars (circle the correct one[s]).

c) How are these changes happening?_____

_____

d) Predict the next element in this series. _____

_____

e) Draw in the next element. Compare your element to the previous ones.
Is the series repeating itself?   Yes / No

2. Check out this pattern.
Write what is drawn in the blank spaces below the drawings.

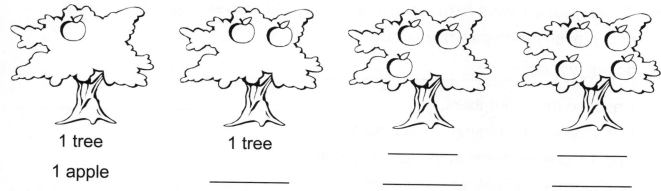

1 tree   1 tree

1 apple   _____   _____   _____

                                   _____   _____

a) In each drawing what was the same? _____

b) What is changing?_____

c) How is it changing? _____

d) Complete these drawings so that they are a part of the series.
Check your work to make sure they are correct.

Activities

Let's check out these number series.

Remember, we are looking for the changes and how they change.

1. 30, 25, 20, _____, _____, _____, _____.

a) These numbers are all_____ .

b) How are the changes taking place? Circle your answer:

increasing by 5s   or   decreasing by 5s

c) Complete the next 4 elements _____, _____, _____, _____.

d) Check your answers.   (i) Are they increasing / decreasing?

(ii) Are they in 5s?   or   Are they not in 5s?

2. 22, 24, 26, 28, _____, _____, _____, _____, _____.

a) These are odd / even numbers.

b) Is the series increasing / decreasing?

c) Go back and fill in the blank spaces.

d) Check your answers to make sure that you have increasing / decreasing

odd / even numbers written down.

3. 99, 88, 77, 66, _____, _____, _____, _____.

a) Describe these numbers._____

b) Is the series increasing / decreasing.

c) Add 4 more elements to the series above.

d) Don't forget to check your answers.

4. Create a series of increasing odd numbers beginning with 5.

a) Start with 5.   b) The next odd number after 5 is _____.

c) _____ is the next odd number after 7.

d) After 9, the next odd number is _____.

e) Write your series here _____

f) Are all of your numbers odd? Yes /No   g) Are the numbers increasing? Yes / No

h) Your series is correct / incorrect.   i) Continue your series until you reach
21.

Year 4: Unit 1
Activities
Here is a mixture of patterns - some increasing, some decreasing.
Complete the patterns.

	The given pattern	Your description of the pattern	The next 3 elements
1.			
2.	12, 15, 18, 21,		
3.	560, 530, 500, 470,		
4.			
5.			
6.	tenth, twelfth, fourteenth,		
7.			
8.	1001, 2001, 3001,		
9.			
10.	30 kg 35 kg 40 kg 45 kg		

Drawing a Picture

By drawing a picture, a problem can often be more easily seen.
We will use pictures/drawings to help solve these.

1. Design a new flag for the country of PROBLEMBA. It is to be 3 vertical, coloured stripes. The national colours of this country are blue, green and red. You could have:

| blue | green | red |

or

| blue | red | green |

or

| red | blue | green |

Colour in the next three in different orders.

| | | | or | | | | or | | | |

As you can see, it's pretty hard to imagine 6 different flags in your mind, but as drawings, it's easy to see.

2. I have 4 squares. How many different shapes can I make with them? Each square must have one side touching another - not just the corners touching.

Let's start some drawings.

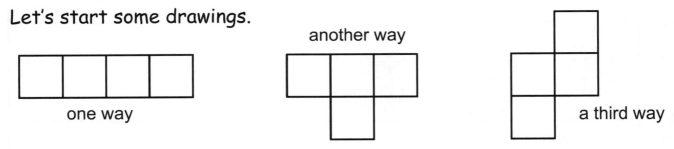

one way   another way   a third way

Add your drawings here. Be careful that your drawing is not the same as any other one if it is turned around!

Activities

For this strategy:

READ   the problem and sort out the information.
DRAW a picture and enter the information on it.
READ   the questions.
USE   the information on the drawing to solve the problem.
CHECK to make sure you are right.

1. Maree has 6 boxes of books. There's a dozen in the first box, 3 less in the second and a score in the third. Five less than the third are in the fourth box and the fifth and sixth boxes each holds one less than the first.
How many books are in all of the boxes?

Read the problem again to make sure you understand it. Draw the boxes.

a) Now enter the information - the number of books on each box.

The first ____, second ____, third ____, fourth ____, fifth ____ and sixth ____.

b) What do we want to find? _____

c) How are we going to find this? _____

d) My answer is _____ books in the six boxes.

e) Check your answer by adding the numbers in a different order.
Is the statement true / false?

f) Answer these questions by looking only at the drawing.

☆ Which box holds the most books? _____

☆ The least books are in box number _____.

☆ The first three boxes contain more / less books than the last three boxes.

☆ Is it possible for box number 2 to be the heaviest? Yes / No. Why? _____

_____

If box number 4 became lost, Maree would have _____ books.

Activities

1. In the library, there is a bookcase with 7 shelves. The bottom shelf has 16 books on it. There are 3 less on the second, 4 more on the third and one more on the fifth. The same number of books as the third shelf are on the sixth shelf, half a dozen on the top shelf and none on the fourth shelf.

	7
	6
	5
	4
	3
	2
	1

Draw the books on the correct shelves then answer the questions.

a) Most books were on the bottom shelf. True / False

b) The least books are on the top shelf. True / False

c) Find the total number of books on the fourth and fifth shelves. _____

d) There are more / less than 50 books in the bookcase.

e) How many books would I need to add to this bookcase so that the total is

exactly 100? _____

2. Rydale School has 4 sports houses. Their colours are blue, red, green and brown. Create as many different flags as you can showing these house colours in different orders. One flag has been done for you.

Blue	Red
Green	Brown

Activities

1. A tank holds 100 litres. It was half full.
    If I used 15 litres of water, how much is left in the tank?

a) Make a quick drawing of the tank in the box.

b) Write how much the tank *can* hold at the top.

c) Colour/shade in how much water was in the tank.

d) Beside the water level, write in how much water was in the tank.

e) Draw a line below the water level to show how much was taken out.

f) Perform the calculation to find out how much is left: _____ litres.

g) Check your answer.

2. Long ago, in a far-off galaxy, was the planet SRAM.
    On this planet lived Goopaloops.
    Goopaloops were unusual, in that every week they doubled their mass.
    At the end of the first week, one Goopaloop had a mass of 1 kg.
    What would this creature's mass be at the end of a six-week period?

a) Here are six panels to represent each week. Finish naming them.

Week 1	Week 2				

b) Draw the Goopaloop in the first panel and write its mass under the drawing.

c) Complete the second panel with a drawing and its mass.

d) Repeat the process for the other panels.

It may be fun drawing a Goopaloop, but don't forget to focus on the real task - to find the correct mass.

e) Finish these statements.

    ☆ At the end of week three the Goopaloop had a mass of _____.

    ☆ The Goopaloop had a mass of 16 kg by the end of week _____.

    ☆ The Goopaloop's mass after 6 weeks was _____.

    ☆ What would this creature weigh after 8 weeks? _____

Activities

1. Use drawings to show at least ten different ways of giving 50 cents as change.

☆ Are these *all* of the possible combinations? Yes / No

2. A roll of material is 45 metres long. From this roll, the haberdasher sold 2 m, 4 m, 3 m, 6 m and 5 m. How much remains on the roll to be sold?

a) On the roll, enter the total length that was on the roll.

b) On the material, mark off the lengths that were sold.

c) How will you solve this problem?_____

_____

d) Find your solution: _____ metres.

e) Check your working and make sure that you've answered the question.

3. On a tall gum tree, there were two big limbs. On each of these limbs there were 4 branches. On each branch there were 3 twigs. On each twig there were 3 leaves. How many leaves were on the tree?

a) Use the space to draw the tree. Draw the limbs, branches and twigs. On one twig draw the three leaves.

b) Work out the total number of:

   (i) limbs _____   (ii) branches _____

   (iii) twigs _____   (iv) leaves _____

Year 4: Unit 2
Activities
Use drawings to help you solve these problems.

Problem	Drawing	Working	Answer
1. Tom's shoes are 2 cm thick. In bare feet, Tom is 147 cm tall. If he lifts his arm straight up, he can reach up another 43 cm. By holding a stick that is 58 cm long, Tom (wearing shoes) can touch an object that is _____ cm off the floor.			
2. A fence is 28 metres long. Fence posts are placed every two metres. This means that I would count _____ posts along this fence.			

3. A room has 4 windows. A lorikeet flew in one window and out a different window. Show as many ways as possible how this could be done.

Use this space to show all of the possible ways. One has been done for you.

in

out

I have been able to draw _____ different possible ways.

How much did you learn?
Try the test on page 62.

Excel Basic Skills *Problem Solving Years 3 - 4*

43

Guessing and Checking

Fred makes 3-legged and 4-legged stools. He has 12 seats and 40 legs. How many of each type of stool can he make by using up all of the items?

Let's make a guess and check it out.

a) Fred has 12 seats so the maximum number of stools he can make is _____.

☆ He could make 6 of each. Let's try that and see what happens.

	1st guess	2nd guess	3rd guess	4th guess
No. of stools with 3 legs	6			
No. of seats	6			
No. of legs	18 (6 × 3)			
No. of stools with 4 legs	6			
No. of seats	6			
No. of legs	24 (6 × 4)			
Total no. of seats	12 (6 + 6)			
Total no. of legs	42 (18 + 24)			
All materials used up?	too many legs			

☆ He can't make 6 of each because he'd need 42 legs. He only has 40 legs in stock. Let's try another guess.

Let's think about this first. He needs to use fewer legs, so he must make more / less 3-legged stools and more / less 4-legged ones.

Let's try seven 3-legged stools and five 4-legged stools.
Go back to the grid and fill in the details.

Is it right? Yes / No

Is it closer? Yes / No

Make another guess, using what you have found out and check it.

b) Fred can make _____ 3-legged stools and _____ 4-legged stools.

Year 4: Unit 3
Activities

1. At the Royal Easter Show, Roger and Dawn saw a cage with chickens and guinea pigs. Roger counted the heads and said there were 21 animals in the cage. Dawn counted the number of legs, which came to a total of 54. Roger told Dawn that from these two numbers he could work out exactly how many of each animal was in the cage. Use guessing and checking to prove Roger was right.

	1st guess	2nd guess	3rd guess	4th guess	5th guess
No. of chickens					
No. of legs					
No. of guinea pigs					
No. of legs					
Total no. of heads					
Total no. of legs					
Correct ✓ Incorrect ✗					

Use these facts. There are 21 animals which means 21 heads.

There were _____ legs.

Make your first guess. Check it. Use your first guess to make a better second guess. Check this. Continue until you find the correct combination for 21 heads and 54 feet.

2. What would the combination be with 21 chickens and guinea pigs but only 44 legs? Complete this table to help you guess and check.

Activities

1. I know of two numbers which, when added together, equal 21.
   If I subtract them the answer is 3. Can you tell me these two numbers?

Let's look at the facts. Added together = 21. Subtracted = 3.

a) My first guess is 6 and 15.

   Add them. 6 + 15 = _____
   Is this true? Yes / No

   Subtract them. 15 – 6 = _____
   Is this true? Yes / No

The numbers should be closer together so that when I subtract them the answer is smaller. Is this statement true / false?

b) A second guess is 8 and 13.

Check

| 8 + 13 = _____ | 13 – 8 = _____ |
| Is it true? Yes / No | Is it closer? Yes / No |

c) A third guess

   is _____.

Check

| | |
| Is it true? Yes / No | Is it closer? Yes / No |

2. Two numbers when added equal 53. When the smaller number is subtracted from the larger number, the answer is 17. Find the missing numbers.
   Record your guesses and checks on this table.

	1st guess	2nd guess	3rd guess	4th guess	5th guess	6th guess
1st number						
2nd number						
Added						
Subtracted						
Right/Wrong						

Remember that these are not wild guesses. After your first guess, you should think about the results and use that information to help you make a better guess the following time.

Activities

Here is the menu at Jack's Diner.

```
· · · · · · · · · · · · · · · · · · · · · ·
:                                          :
:   Jack's Diner                           :
:                                          :
:   Burgers $3.20                          :
:   Cheeseburger..............$2.50        :
:   Small drink..................$1.20      :
:   Large drink ..................$1.80     :
:   Chips    regular ............$1.50      :
:              large ...............$2.00   :
:   Ice-cream .........................60   :
:   Sundae .....................$1.60       :
:                                          :
· · · · · · · · · · · · · · · · · · · · · ·
```

a) Paul purchased two items.
    He received 90 ¢ change from a
    $5.00 note.
    Which two items did he purchase?

(1st guess) | Check |

(2nd guess) | Check |

b) Cassie made 3 purchases.
    Her bill came to $5.80.
    Which items did she buy?

Cassie:	1st guess	2nd guess	3rd guess	4th guess	5th guess	6th guess
Item one						
Item two						
Item three						
Total cost						
Check: ✓ or ✗						

c) Mr Rodrigez purchased 4 different items from the menu. His total cost was
    six dollars and eighty cents. Use guessing and checking to find out the four
    items he purchased.

Mr Rodrigez:	1st guess	2nd guess	3rd guess	4th guess	5th guess	6th guess
Item one						
Item two						
Item three						
Item four						
Total cost						
Check: ✓ or ✗						

Activities

1. In the carpark, Lucia saw trucks with six wheels
   and cars (with 4 wheels). She told me it would take
   11 drivers to get all of those 50 wheels moving at once.
   'Bet you can't tell me the exact number of trucks
   there,' she said. Help me prove that I can.

	1st guess	2nd guess	3rd guess	4th guess	5th guess	6th guess
Trucks						
Truck wheels						
Cars						
Car wheels						
Total wheels						
Check: ✓ or ✗						

2.
a) Tran has 60 cents more than me. Li has 10 cents less than me.
   If we pool all of our money, we have a total of $4.40.
   Your task is to be a detective to find out how much money I have, given only
   these facts.

Tran						
Li						
Me						
Total						
Check: ✓ or ✗						

Now that you've solved that, see if you can quickly complete this
problem.

b) If, when we (Tran, Li and me) pooled our money, the total was $4.70, how
   much did we each have?

   Tran $_____, Li $_____ and me $_____.

Activities

Here are some problems. Use guessing and checking to solve them. Set up your own guess and check grids in the space provided. Don't forget to check your final guess to make sure it is right.

1. Last year, we visited the zoo at Dubbo. In one enclosure we saw wombats and kangaroos. Mum said that she saw 48 big and strong legs on these animals. Dad said that the enclosure was a good size for the 18 animals. Given these clues, work out the number of each of these mammals.

My answer is _____.

2. Find the 'magic' numbers. When I add these two numbers the total is ninety-nine. The larger number minus the smaller number gives a difference of twenty-seven. The two numbers are both less than a hundred and your task is to find them.

My answer is _____.

How much did you learn?
Try the test on page 63.

Year 4: Unit 4
Working Backwards

1. I had some money. I spent $40 on two CDs. Mrs Rafter offered me some odd jobs to do.
   After doing the jobs, I was paid $20. I counted up the money I now had and found a total of $65.
   How much did I have before I bought the CDs?

Let's start at the end and work backwards.

a) I ended up with $_____ in my wallet.

b) Mrs Rafter paid me $_____.

c) This means that before Mrs Rafter paid me I had $_____.

d) I spent $_____ purchasing the CDs.

e) To find how much I had before buying the CDs, I will have to add / subtract

   $_____ and $_____.

f) This means I had $_____ in my wallet to start with.

Don't forget to put this answer into the problem. Work the problem forwards to check that your answer is correct.

2. When Barbara got out of bed she forgot to look at the thermometer, but it was really cold. By midday the temperature had risen 12°C to a reasonable level, but by 4 p.m. the temperature had fallen back 8°C to a chilly 6°C. If Barbara had checked the thermometer that morning, the reading would have been a very cold _____ degrees Celsius.

Let's track the changes backwards.

a) At 4 p.m. the temperature was _____.

b) The temperature fell by _____ degrees between midday and 4 p.m.

c) This means that the temperature at midday must have been _____ degrees.

d) During the morning, the temperature rose by _____ degrees.

e) Will I add / subtract this rise to / from the midday temperature?

f) Therefore, the morning temperature was _____ degrees.

g) Describe how you checked your work. _____

1. From his stack of NBA collector cards, Marc traded 36 of his duplicate cards to Paula for 19 cards he didn't have. Marc then counted up his cards - five less than a hundred. Before trading, he had _____ more than a hundred.

   ☆ Steps I took to solve this

   _____

   _____

   _____

   _____

   _____

   My answer is _____.

   ☆ How I proved my answer.

   _____

   _____

2. On the Wild Ride pinball machine you can win or lose points for each of the three balls. I won points on the first ball. I lost 3000 on the second ball. 5000 points were won on the third ball, giving me a total score of 9000 points. Just how many points did I win on the first ball?

   ☆ This is how I worked this problem out.

   _____

   _____

   _____

   _____

   On the first ball I won _____ points.

   ☆ This is the way I proved that my answer is right.

   _____

   _____

Activities

1. Andrea rolled two dice three times.
   Her total score for the three rolls was 26.
   Her last roll was an eleven.
   Her second roll was five less than her third roll.
   Her second roll was three less than her first roll.
   Her scores were: _____ 1st roll; _____ 2nd roll; _____ 3rd roll. Total of 26.

Here we could use guessing and checking but let's stick to working backwards to find our answers.

a) Andrea's last roll was_____.

b) Her second roll was_____ more / less than the third roll.

c) This means her second score was_____.

d) The first roll was_____ more / less than the second.

e) Calculate the score on the first roll. _____

f) Let's prove that. Add all three rolls. The total is _____, which means our

   answers are correct / incorrect.

2. Only 100 tickets were made available for the rock concert.
   All were sold in 3 hours.
   The last 26 were sold in the third hour.
   Nine more than that were sold during the second hour of sales.
   The first hour was even higher, with four more than the second hour being sold.
   How many tickets were sold each hour?

a) In the last hour _____ were sold.

b) In the second hour the total was _____ than the third.

c) This means that _____ were sold in the second hour.

d) First hour sales were _____ than the second hour.

e) By my figuring, _____ tickets were sold in the first hour.

f) My three answers are _____ (1st hour), _____ (2nd hour), _____ (3rd hour).

g) This is how I proved my answers are correct. _____

_____

The four steps to problem solving are SEE, PLAN, DO and CHECK.
All steps are really important.

Excel Basic Skills *Problem Solving Years 3 - 4*

Activities

1. Read this problem carefully. (SEE)
   At the ape display at Taronga Park, I counted 8 big gorillas. My brother said that there were 13 more chimpanzees than there were great apes. My sister said, 'Well, I counted eleven more monkeys than you counted chimpanzees.' Dad asked, 'Given those facts, just how many animals did you all count?'

   a) How are you going to solve this problem? (PLAN) _____

   _____

   b) Just how did you solve it? (DO)_____

   _____

   _____

   _____

   c) Your answer to the problem is _____ animals.

   d) How did you prove your answer? (CHECK) _____

   _____

2. SEE (read carefully)
   Harvey, Val and Gloria were playing darts. Gloria scored 32 with her three darts. Val scored 26 more than Gloria and 16 more than Harvey.
   Arrange the people with their scores in order from highest to lowest.

   a) PLAN (how to do it) _____

   _____

   b) DO (solve the problem) _____

   _____

   _____

   _____

   c) Answer is_____

   d) CHECK (prove you are right)_____

   _____

It's a great feeling to know that you not only have an answer to a problem, but the answer you have is right!

Acting It Out

1. Karen has some dollar coins. If she makes stacks of 5 coins, one will be left over. If she makes stacks of 4 coins, all stacks will be equal. Looking at the heap, she knows that there are more than ten coins but not enough to make $20. How much does Karen have?

We could use guessing or checking or we could use a number of 'coins' (counters) and actually make the stacks.

Use less than 20 counters (we know this from reading the problem).

a) Make one stack of 5 with one over. Will this work? Yes / No

   Why? _____

b) Let's try two stacks of 5 with one over. Is it between 10 and 20? Yes / No

c) Make that number into stacks of 4 coins. Are the stacks equal with none left

   over? Yes / No

d) If that didn't work, you'll have to try _____

e) This number makes _____ stacks of 5 with _____ left over.

f) Use that number of 'coins' to make stacks of 4. Are these stacks all equal

   with none left over? Yes / No

g) From your trials so far, only one is correct: _____ 'coins'.

h) Would 4 stacks of 5 'coins' with one left over work? Yes / No

   Why? _____

i) This means that there's only one correct answer: _____ 'coins'.

j) Karen has $_____ in one dollar coins.

We don't have to check this problem at the end because we have been checking as we worked through the problem. We found only one number that fitted the conditions in the problem so we know this answer is correct.

2. If the heap of coins was valued between $30 and $40 (and the same conditions applied), Karen would have exactly $_____.

   Use the same process with your counters to find the one number which will give you stacks of 5 with 1 over or equal stacks of 4. Draw your stacks here.

Activities

1. Arrange these people in order - tallest to shortest - given this information.
   Herb is not as tall as Harry. Harry is taller than both Hans and Henry.
   Hans isn't as tall as Henry but is taller than Herbert.

Make name cards for the 4 people: Herbert, Henry, Harry and Hans.

☆ Place them in an order.

☆ Check your order with the information given in the problem.

☆ If the information doesn't fit, re-arrange the 'people'.

☆ Check the new order with the problem. If it doesn't fit, re-arrange.

☆ Continue until you find the right order.

Record your trials here.

a) _____   d) _____

b) _____   e) _____

c) _____   f) _____

The only order which fits the problem is: _____

2. Don climbed up a mossy, slippery bank. It was hard work. After 10 minutes,
   he had climbed up 3 metres. As he rested for 2 minutes he slid back one
   metre. If he continues like this, it will take him _____ minutes to reach the
   top of this 11 metre bank.

Use a counter to represent Don. You'll need an oblique number line to represent the mossy bank.

Mark off 11 'metre' marks on the line.

a) Move the counter up 3 metres.   This took _____ minutes.

b) Slide the counter back 1 metre.   Add _____ minutes.

c) Move the counter up 3 metres.   This equals _____ minutes.

d) Slide it back 1 metre.   Another _____ minutes.

e) Up another 3 metres.   Add _____ minutes.

f) Back down he slides.   Again _____ minutes.

g) Has he reached the top yet?   Yes / No

h) Up another 3 metres.   Add _____ minutes.

i) Has he reached the top now?   Yes / No

j) Add all of the times you've recorded.   _____ minutes.

Activities

1. You were on the bus with 6 other people. At the first stop, 3 got on the bus and 1 got off. Four on, 1 off at the next stop. At the third stop, 2 on, 5 off. At the next stop, 2 ladies and a man got on after 3 children got off. There are now _____ people on the bus.

To help you solve this problem, you can use counters to represent people.

a) How many people were on the bus at the start? _____

b) 1st stop: add those who got on. Now there are _____ people.

c) Take off the number who got off the bus there. _____ people left.

d) 2nd stop: Add on the people who got on the bus. _____ people.

e) Subtract those who got off the bus. There are now _____ on the bus.

f) 3rd stop: Add those that got on. Take off those who left the bus.

   This means there are _____ people on the bus.

g) 4th stop: _____ on and _____ off leaves _____ people on the bus.

Check your adding and subtracting to make sure your totals are correct.

2. This problem is much like the first one, but instead of being written in words, it is a drawing. Use similar steps to above to find the answers.

32 people	10 on 5 off	6 on 8 off	16 on 3 off	4 on 10 off	?
	1st station	2nd station	3rd station	4th station	

a) _____

b) _____

c) _____

d) _____

e) _____

f) _____

g) Proof: _____

h) As the train left the fourth station there were _____ people on board.

Year 4: Unit 5
Activities

Solve these using counters to act it out.

1. SEE   Graham has between $4 and $3 in ten cent coins. If he makes stacks of 50 cents, he has 2 coins left over. If he makes stacks of 40 cents, he uses all the coins and has none left over.

   PLAN   a) I will solve this by _____

   _____

   DO   b) This is how I solved this problem _____

   _____

   _____

   c) Graham has $_____.

   CHECK d) How I checked my working and answer._____

   _____

2. Three best friends each have different jobs. Here's what I know about them. You work out their ages and their occupations.

   ☆ Carlo is younger than Maria.   ☆ Guiseppi is a mechanic.
   ☆ The oldest is a bank manager.   ☆ The plasterer is younger than the mechanic.

Name	Age	Occupation

3. Kerry, Rupert, John and Rose are all very rich people. Arrange them in order from the person with the most wealth to the one with the least money.

   ☆ Rupert is a great deal richer than John.
   ☆ Kerry is far richer than Rose, almost as rich as Rupert.
   ☆ John could buy all of Rose's assets and still have some money left over.

1st trial _____, _____, _____, _____.   check yes / no

2nd trial _____, _____, _____, _____.   check yes / no

3rd trial _____, _____, _____, _____.   check yes / no

How much did you learn?
Try the test on page 64.

Creating a Table
To use this strategy you'll need to:

☆ Know what information is given.

☆ Make a table to show the results.

☆ Enter the information on the table.

☆ Check to make sure that you haven't left anything out.

How many different numbers can I create using the digits 1, 3, 5 and 7?

With 4 digits I will be able to make 4 different groups of numbers in the thousands place. So let's make a table with 4 headings.

one thousands	three thousands	five thousands	_____ thousands

a) Let's see what numbers can be made in the one thousands. 1357 is one, 1375 is a second. 1537 a third and 1573 a fourth. Find the fifth _____ and sixth _____ numbers.

b) In the three thousands I found 3157, 3175 and 3517. You find the other numbers in this group. _____, _____ and _____.

c) Find all of the 6 numbers in the five thousands: _____, _____, _____, _____, _____ and _____.

d) Find the numbers in the seven thousands range: _____, _____, _____, _____, _____ and _____.

e) Enter each of these groups into the table above. Record the numbers in order - smallest to largest in each section of the table.

Putting them in order is more logical than mixing them up. If you ever have to refer to this table, then being in order will make it much easier to use. Answer these questions.

f) Which number is the closest to 7500? _____.

g) From the table above, find the numbers which lie between 3000 and 3500:

_____, _____.

h) Write the five thousands numbers in descending order. _____, _____,

_____, _____, _____, _____.

Activities

1. Every minute a machine makes a dozen whirligigs.

Let's show this production rate on a table.

Time (minutes)	1	2	3	4	5	6	7			
No. of whirligigs		24	36			72				

a) Some of the table is filled in, you complete the rest.

b) Now use the table to answer these questions.

☆ In 5 minutes, _____ whirligigs will be made.

☆ To make 96 whirligigs the machine will take _____ minutes.

☆ After ten minutes _____ dozen whirligigs will be made.

☆ 3 score of whirligigs take _____ minutes to make.

☆ Whirligigs are packed in boxes of 24. If the machine makes these items

for 8 minutes, _____ boxes will be needed to pack them in.

2. 'I think Paul is foolish to take a job which pays 1 dollar the first day, 2 dollars the second, 4 dollars the third, and then continues doubling each day. After a fortnight he will have earned hardly anything at all,' said Sharma in disgust.

Is Paul really foolish? Finish off this table and check it out.

Week 1 – Days	1	2		4	5		7
Earnings	$1	$2	$4	$8			
Week 2 – Days	8		10				14
Earnings							

a) On the seventh day, Paul will be paid _____ .

b) Paul earns $512 on the _____ day.

c) During the whole of the first week Paul only earns _____ .

d) On the last day of the fortnight, Paul will be paid _____ .

e) Work out the total amount he will be paid for the 14 days. _____

f) Was Paul really foolish or not? _____

Creating a List

Making a list in an organised way can help you find all of the possibilities in a situation. Check these out.

Peta has 3 tops (red, white, blue), 4 skirts (grey, black, blue, red) and 3 pairs of shoes (tan, navy, black). By mixing and matching (changing at least one item), Peta can create _____ different outfits.

Let's take each top one at a time and find combinations for that top.

a)   Red top, grey skirt and tan shoes is the first combination (1, 1, 1)

b)   Now change the shoes - red top, grey skirt, navy shoes (1, 1, 2)

c)   A third outfit is red top, grey skirt and _____ shoes (1, 1, 3)

d)   Now change a skirt - red top, black skirt and tan shoes (1, 2, 1)

e)   Now the shoes again - red top, black skirt and _____ shoes (1, 2, 2)

f)   The next combination is _____ top, _____ skirt and _____ shoes (1, 2, 3)

g)   Change skirt again - red top, blue skirt and tan shoes (1, 3, 1)

h)   Shoes again - red top, blue skirt and _____ shoes (1, 3, 2)

i)   The next logical combination is _____ (1, 3, 3)

There are three more possible combinations with a red top. Write them.

j)   _____ top, _____ skirt, _____ shoes (1, 4, 1)

k)   _____ top, _____ skirt, _____ shoes (1, 4, 2)

l)   _____ top, _____ (1, 4, 3)

m) With a red top there are _____ possible combinations.

n)   List all the combinations Peta can make with her white top.

Skirt	Shoes	Skirt	Shoes

o)   With the red top she created _____ combinations.

p)   With her white top she had _____ different outfits to wear.

q)   Estimate how many outfits she can create with her blue top. _____

r)   On a separate sheet, prove that your estimate is right / wrong.

s)   Now calculate just how many outfits she can create by mixing and matching all of these items.

Activities

Solve these problems. Lists will help.

1. **SEE** Make a list of all of the possible meals you can create by choosing one main meal and one dessert from this take-away menu.

   ☆ Pizza   ☆ Ice-cream
   ☆ Burger   ☆ Cheesecake
   ☆ Chicken & Chips ☆ Custard
   ☆ Fish & Chips   and fruit

PLAN How are you going to solve this? _____

_____

DO				
CHECK	Make sure you have included all possible combinations.			

2. Here's Mum's shopping and 'to do' list. Reorganise the list into groups, then order the groups to make the most logical listing possible. Here are the shops she will need to visit:

   home   baker   butcher   hair-dresser   supermarket

a) Here are the groupings I made:

☆ _____

☆ _____

☆ _____

☆ _____

Mum's list

☆ butter   ☆ sugar
☆ mince   ☆ soft drink
☆ detergent   ☆ milk
☆ flour   ☆ sausages
☆ peanuts   ☆ steak
☆ collect bag of dog bones
☆ 2 loaves of bread
☆ 6 fresh pies
☆ get hair trim
☆ collect birthday cake

b) Mum should go first to the _____
   then do the rest of her shopping in this order (give reasons): _____

_____

_____

How much did you learn?
Try the test on page 65.

Year 4:
Test 1
Finding a Pattern and Drawing a Picture

Check out how well you can find a pattern or draw a picture to help solve these.

1. Work out what comes next in these.

   a) 70, 63, 56, 49, _____, _____, _____, _____.

   b) △ , △ , △ , △ , △ , △ , △ ,   ,   ,   ,   .

   c) 42, 44, 46, 48, 50, _____, _____, _____, _____.

   d) 101, 202, 303, 404, _____, _____, _____, _____.

2. I have 3 counters (one red, one white, one black).
   Show the different ways you can arrange them.

3. Dad had a 50 kg bag of fertiliser. He used 10 kg on Monday and half the remainder of Tuesday. This left _____ kg to use on Wednesday.
   Show a drawing and describe how you solved this.

a) Drawing	b) How I did it.
	c) Answer = _____

4. Use different coloured pencils to show different routes Fido can take to get to his kennel through the breaks in the fence.

There are _____ ways.

62   Excel Basic Skills *Problem Solving Years 3 - 4*

Test 2

Guessing and Checking

Let's see how well you can use Guessing and Checking to solve these.

1. In the bike store there were bicycles and unicycles (only one wheel).
    I counted 22 seats and 42 wheels. How many of each were there?

Check						

2. Oranges cost 20 cents. Apples are worth 15 cents. I spent $2.60 on 15
    pieces of fruit. I bought _____ oranges and _____ apples.

Check						

3. Pete picked two numbers. He added them: 81. He subtracted them: 37.
    The two numbers were _____ and _____.

Check						

Test 3
Working Backwards and Acting It Out

Use either Working Backwards or Acting It Out to find the answers to these problems.

1. Gail is shorter than Ross but taller than Marie.
Ross is not as tall as John but Ross is 12 cm above Marie.
Gail is as tall as Ross when she is wearing shoes and he is in bare feet.
Use this information to arrange the people from shortest to tallest.

_____

2. When Brett was sick he lost 23 kg. Since then, he has put on 8 kg and now

weighs 74 kg. What was Brett's weight before he got sick? _____

3. Describe how you would solve this problem. No solution is required.
I had some money in my wallet. I purchased some items for $20. Dad gave me $15. I just counted my money, and I have exactly $50.

How much did I have before? _____

_____

_____

4. Which strategy would be best to use to solve this?_____

In a foot race,
   ☆ Jill beat Bill by 1 metre.
   ☆ Phil was 2 metres in front of Bill.
   ☆ Lill came in 2 metres after Jill.

b) How would you go about solving this? _____

_____

c) My answer is _____

d) How would you check this? _____

_____

5. Of my flock of racing pigeons, 16 flew away. After I purchased 10 more, I

then had 52 in my flock. Originally I had _____ pigeons.

_____

_____

_____

Test 4
Make a List and Make a Table

Make a list or table to help in solving these.

1. Mum gave me the choice of white, brown or wholemeal bread with either ham, chicken or lamb filling. I said I'd have one of each. How many sandwiches did Mum make for me?

2. A kilogram of peanuts costs $1.50.

a) Complete this table, then answer the questions.

Kilogram	1	2	3	4	5	6	7	8	9	10	11
Cost											

b) I spent $6 and bought _____ kg of peanuts.

c) 7 kg will cost me $_____.

d) Do 9 kg of peanuts cost $12? Yes / No

e) If 10 kg costs $_____, then 20 kg will cost _____.

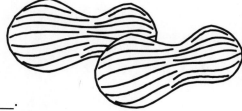

3. Ice-cream comes in vanilla (v), strawberry (s), chocolate (c), caramel (k), rainbow (r) and mango (m).

   a) If I have a double (2 different flavours) each day, it will take me _____ days to try every combination.

   b) Prove your answer by showing the combinations. One is done for you.

Notes